Introduction

I began to write poetry after my son's
earnest after my mom died in 2000. I needed words to help me
express inner groaning, sadness, and the type of joy felt when the
cardinal sings. Being in nature helped sooth and gave me words.

I started taking poetry classes at the Loft in 2002 with an excellent
poet, Juliet Patterson, who then became my mentor. She
recommended me for the Master's Program at Hamline University
in St. Paul, Minnesota in 2003. I took my first poetry course in the
fall of that year from poet Deborah Keenan. Deborah
commissioned us on the first night to be poets, to observe the earth
and our lives and to write poetry.

I took her commissioning seriously and have taken a closer look
outside of myself, at the earth and her creatures around me in the
first section of this collection: *Earth*. Nature holds a wisdom of
her own. The bird's song has given me strength in times of
sorrow, the winter tree has lent her ear.

In the second section: *Kin*, I have looked more closely within
myself, to write about the person I am and about my kin, who are a
part of me. A guest author told our class, "Never be ashamed of
anything you write." This has called me to write about my life
more honestly. I explore life growing up in a large family with its
ups and downs. I also wrestle with the hurts and joys of life as a
spouse and mother. Please come inside, welcome to my world and
may it intersect with yours.

Of Earth

"The province of the poem is the world. When the sun rises in the poem and when it sets darkness comes down and the poem is dark." William Carlos Williams, *Paterson*

My Goddess

wears a crescent and

two

stars.

She puts the spark in pitch

dark.

Darkness formidable

in the room

she brushes past

and serves dawn

at long last

to hungry hearts,
stuck at midnight.

Starlight -filled her faithful
tell their stories.

Her tear,
the last star
to leave the sky

Her laughter

a belly full of pink.

Sugar Maple

A tree in fall I like best of all is
maple, sugar maple.

Her shapely leaves of orange, yellow, red when sun shine and she wed merely
silken scarves slipping from her shoulders.

Fitting is the earthy, musky fragrance she leaves behind as memories
remind me of the backyard leaf pile and being buried in that smell like mama's
underarm.

Shadows on her trunk foreshadowing what's to come for today,
crisp air makes me take notice.

Life Paced Prayer

Help us to never live so fast

As to miss the reflection of a yellow willow

On a lake of glass.

Future's Hope

On a branch

One cone

Cries out

Amid a tree of pine

Future's Hope

Cricket Song

Crickets below my window this morn
Sound like the crickets that sang me to sleep
Their serenade simple, a regulated be-be-beat
Goes back from birth to October

Their mantra melody memory holds dear
A comfort like Dad's snore when I woke at night
Or the tock of the grandfather clock
When sleeping over at Grandma's

Like a hurting bird held in my small hand
The cricket song, like walking on warm sand
I look forward to each year
Don't want to miss a word

The Robin Couple

Couples promenading on the back lawn
Several levels to their intonation
Sassy, "That was my worm for the kids,"
To serenading song when belly's full.

Your breast the color of a full-figured oak
The song you sing early morning lilts
When you leave stark stillness fills the air
Not unlike a spouse's silent treatment.

The Mouse

I would just as soon
give up my house
to the most unwelcome mouse
who entered by a crevice last week

He avoids every trap we set
boldly he comes out to let
little ones and uncourageous mother
know he's there

He is hard to predict
he's fast and easily picks
a night run, racing claws heard
like fingernails on chalkboards

We will hire an exterminator
to relieve us, for this vermin hater
can no longer stomach
the unpredictable

Summer Morning

Sunlight shines on cardinal's red coat as he perches on the garden fence.
Droplets of water wink green and blue
like tiny bubbles on blades of grass.

Robins sing songs from tree to tree
Offering their musical background
To our simple conversation.

As we have breakfast on the screen porch
In the cool air. Rain chased away the humidity.
Eating fresh strawberry jam on toast and strong coffee with cream.

Dawn and Atlas

Dawn, thick band of brilliant light
Like Atlas
Holds up the Ominous
Gray cloud

Hurling it towards Wisconsin
Where it will dump trucks
Of wet snow

Leaving this March day
In a suit of white fur
And pine.

The Tree

Squatty
Fir Tree
Covered in snow
Whipped cream on dessert
Perfect

First
Real Tree

Round and Round
They uncoil blue,
Yellow   red   green
G u m d r o p s   s t r i n g
T h e   l i g h t s.
Pine scent sticky on fingers.

"Let's plug it in,"
Smiles light up
The tree.

Robin

Herald

of Spring

On top of barren Maple

Sing like you

don't care

What other people think

Inscription for the Entrance to the Wooded Path

Bring your "tired to the bone" spirit
Breathe in rain
Let the pale breeze kiss your cheeks

How you look means nothing here
Cardinal sings his crimson song
To an audience of you

Birch still white from winter
Holds hands with green and leafy
Arms raised in adoration

Against the azure sky
Grassy fields look empty
And muskrat ribbons sketch a pond

The Backside

Around the house where the screened porch lives
is the spare key hiding for the faithful few.

A simple strand of clothesline holds his blue and her peach
teacher shirts and a "Just Do It" tennis tee from the dear son they had late.

A favorite time from April to October around a simple table
is hearing the family stories of their day's highs and lows

Neighbors to the porch, the dryer exhaust burred in lint
and the radon pipe, stick out like white hairs in eyebrows.

And what about the R2D2 central air cylinder
Three times bigger than a student's desk?

Drain pipes drape like unhooked bras
while white stones grow better than flowers.

Six foot guard fence knights the vegetables
rabbits never taste and she still thinks it's "Ridiculous."

The grill that once donned a black cape now stands
naked.

The old bird feeder leans in to welcome the red-headed finch
who places import on seeds and singing.

Six pines giant a family from peering eyes and offer castle
for nesting songbirds.

Robin's soprano, operas through the opened kitchen window.
out front showy perennials receive guests.

Blue Heron, Loon

One trolls the edge
Another dives deep in the middle
Of a velvet lake

Slender legs move
In measured step
Measured step

While a white chest and pointed bill
Peer the depths for food
Soon to dive

Graceful steps and grey blue feathers
Pointed grace along the shore
Both stab the same order of fish

Distinction of delicate feathers favored in women's hats
Brought one to near extinction
Life lived far enough north keeps others' haunting melody alive

Chickadees

Small, black and white like wait staff
feathered beings with tiny claws
Dart in and out, branch to skeletal branch
And sing, sing to me
Though they don't even know me
Why do beings who know each other fail to sing to each other?

Summer Wears

a full-brimmed straw hat
        rimmed in spicy marigolds
                frosted in sunshine

her sleeves of monarch lace
        ruffle as she steps lightly
                through rows of
                        blushing tomatoes
                                swollen plump eggplant
                                        and tastes basil's sweet burst

bending to pick pale blue morning glories
        she places them in the crevice of her breast
                still dripping dew

tiny golden finch speaks harshly
        as she dances with red, yellow and orange zinnias
                disturbing their repose and his morning repast

as she lays among the sweet basil
        intoxicated with the scent
                cardinal and cicadas seranade

her straw hat fallen
        carries with it
                summer's scent

A Blessing for the Black Hills of South Dakota

Pine studded rock slabs
Hair pin turns kissed by forests
Crystal clear lakes, trout

Buffalo grazing
Antelope crossing the road
Heads up prairie dogs

Granite faces of presidents
Crazy horse mountain
Staying at the lodge

A walk beside a crystal lake
For two lake trout we named
Walter and Grace

For a Stonehenge rock formation
Outlining Sylvan Lake
For blueberry pancake mornings

Majestic pines stand guard
Beside the highways
As we gratefully bid goodbye.

581 is Stepping Out

May to June belong to home remodeling!
Outside, workers tear off the forty-year-old siding and gutters
And wrap the home in protective plastic

Anderson windows fill in the fresh-aired openings
An explosion rocks the family while eating supper
A mother mallard flew head-long and unaware of the crystal clear pane

 As the lilacs pop, saws begin to cut sheets of Savannah wicker siding
Workers measure and nail each piece in place
With the care of a seamstress sewing her quilt

The hickory red roof becomes a wide-brimmed hat worn with a new poplin suit
A scarlet red door, the silk scarf splash of color
581 is stepping out of her tired ordinary clothes

Inside she wears intimate apparel of shaker beige, bone white, scarlet oak and ember
Bedrooms, hallway, living room and entry burst in contrasting shades
Spouses like an oxen team, brush and roll, brush and roll rouge to cheeks

Artist friend arrives and original watercolors, family photos and precious saints
Are hung like favorite jewels
Saturday morning coffee eases aches as they smile proudly at a midlife makeover

Newly poured cement leads guests and family
Along a path of spiky bee balm, stella lily cups and the scent of roses
Into opened arms of welcome

Of Kin

I Come From

I come from the prairie on Saddle Hill
that greets me as I return home on Highway 14.

I come from the shores of the Missouri River
I swam in summers as a kid and nearly drowned.

I come from playing baseball with brothers on capital lawns
and hearing geese honk overhead on their way to Capital Lake.

I come from 111 N. Nicollet, 224-4879 was our home phone.
We looked across the street and saw the capitol's dome.

I come from walks to confession on Saturdays with Dad,
St. Peter and Paul Catholic Church and filling up a pew on Sunday.

I'm from the smell of Mom and Dad's dressing on Thanksgiving eve.
Onions and celery sautéing in real butter, we left our beds for a whiff.

I'm from Aunt Ruth's cherry pie and big-as-plates sugar cookies
Green and red frosting so sweet, we were begging for more.

I come from fear of the dark, leaving a light on,
sleeping with older sisters and the comfort of parents praying
        each night in the room next door.

Batter Up

Mark always pitches.
He's my younger brother with an ace arm.
You want him on your team.

"Batter up," my brother Tim, the catcher, calls.
He can tag a runner at home and hurl the ball to second base
for a double play. He's another younger brother.

"Back it up, we've got a hitter!" catcher yells to the infield.
I step away from my position at third base into the shallow edge of left field,
crouched and ready for the hit.

As Ralph, younger brother by two years, strides up to home plate,
I ask myself, "Who gave that guy a bat?"
Swoosh, he misses Mark's curve. "Strike one!"

"Give him your fast pitch," I telepath Mark.
Pitcher throws. It ticks off the old blonde bat.
"Fowl ball," Tim yells for us to hear.

I watch as Ralph squares his solid legs and pulls the bat back.
Fear aches in my belly as I ready for his hit.
"Thuunk," the hard ball leaves his bat and hurls meteor-like towards my head.

I duck. Left fielder misses. It rolls to the fence.
Knees still quaking, I relay the ball from outfield towards home plate.
I catch that smirk instead, as Ralph rounds third base and makes it home.

Ralph

His swimming trunks whispered "chubby"
Brother and sister,
Entered beginning summer swimming class.

His fourth grade confidence a buoy
Led him to say, "I'll do the test first."
My sixth grade uncertainty, a lead necklace wearing me down.

The final test, across freezing pool in the park and back
Sent my dread sweating down
Like when going up the hill to confession on Saturday night.

Hardly winded Ralph finished the test
And had air left to offer me encouragement.

"You can do it!" His voice my beacon
When water blinded and air was scarce.

My lungs near bursting, I touched the concrete pool wall
His grin, as I cleared the water's surface,
"We passed!"

Sis

Your invitation came that stifling week in June.

"Bring my nephew." You'd heard the sound of my lonely heart.

Small boy and his mom traveled across state lines, MN to SD
like kids on a mission for ice cream.

That first breakfast, at table, you bent down close to him, eyes looking into eyes.

Gently you cut peanut-buttered toast into toddler squares.

"Let's go swimming after breakfast," you told him in that impish voice.

His response, a broad smile, his eyes a bright "yes."

"Your mom's going shopping, we'll stay and play."

You nodded permission for me to go.

I shut the door and recalled another time you, sis, included me.

Remember Shelley your friend, the only friend on the block, who had the playhouse with red and white checkered curtains?

"Come play with us," your words to me.

Grandma's Ear

Held my high school secrets
The summer of my junior year

From your California home you flew to us
Your son's large Midwestern brood

As I leaned in to hug the Grandma I hardly knew
I sensed safety in your neck of talcum flowers.

A week of visits, your brandy at night to "help your knees,"
Made you real, a relative whose heart held time.

You'd lean in close enough
For my tear of inadequacy to wet your lobe

A prom with no date
My feminine worth at stake

Your nod and words reassuring
"You are more than someone's date"

Now Grandmother Maple
Your shawl of yellowing branches

Holds a sweet heavy fragrance of dried leaves
I lean into

The elder who's trusted ear again
Receives secrets

Sister Second Oldest

She taught me how to cream sugar and shortening for fresh peach pie
that summer following my freshman year of college.

"Use the back of the spoon and press the sugar into the shortening
against the wall of that chipped ceramic mixing bowl."

The sun through her lone kitchen window above the sink
illumined our work like a highlighter on the page shouts, "Important."

In age a decade older, she'd been like a mom when our mom was occupied with
four younger brothers who emptied mom's energy like her change purse.

Norma, a full time worker with three teenagers
took time to impart sweet cooking basics whose finale dripped down my cheek.

She sensed my heart resembled her jewelry box
empty of valuables like attention.

Her back sliding door opened to the kitchen as I stopped on my way back to college
I was wrapped in the smell of cake.

Norma had invited me to stop by for lunch of a roast beef sandwich laced with mayo.
Dad had died a month earlier and she peeked into the empty room of my heart.

Her, "How's college?" and chocolate frosting on my tongue soothed
Like a mother's voice after a bad dream.

Sing Me a Lullaby

for Mom

Under the yellow aspen
Outstretched branches
protecting me.

We talked about your grandson,
in first grade,
now.

And son-in-law,
we are in counseling
yet.

You, I see rocking Ken
Singing, "Glory Halleluia,"
then.

Please,
sing me a lullaby.

"To make a difference in one person's life is immensely more precious than the value of the whole world." St. Peter Canisius

Precious
for Mom

Last time I saw you
you'd fallen at sis Norma's home.
Pushed out of the hospital
too soon after cancer surgery.

Eighty-two,
your badly bruised face winced
as you smiled greeting
upon my arrival.

Next day was the only day
I've spent alone
with you.

You beamed stories
of dating Dad,
your college sweetheart.

I wrote them down
on green memo paper
the nurse loaned me.

Sad, I'd dropped high school Shorthand.
I couldn't write fast enough,
your every word.

First Family Vacation

for Dad

'Til eighth grade I didn't like you.
Disciplinarian with a belt.
Never sharing your plate of food, like Mom.

Then we took our first family vacation.
Stopping for breakfast
you told the youngest,

"Have a tall stack and large milk!"

"The more a thing is torn, the more places it can connect."
Meredith Stricker, *Island*

Father

Knew best behind his paper.
Introverts need time to hide
from toddler spills and teenage woes.

The year we drove to Riggs High
prairie waved, my best friend moved.
I cried tears of abandonment.
A dad I never knew lent me his hanky.

Vatican II changed a church.
Daily drives to highschool
changed us.

After my car accident in college
I saw you as the emergency room doors parted.
You wiped a tear away quickly.
Your eyes reassured, your warm hand held mine.

Colors I Will Miss

Smoking crayons like pretend cigarettes with my sis Marge
        in her friend Shelly's playhouse

Avocado green appliances in her kitchen
        Mr. Coffee brewing up a visit with Mom

Dad's rust robe hugging me home
        From a rough week of finals at college

"You're beautiful," in my teal silk dress, spoken by fiancée Art
        the night we announced our engagement at a Christmas party

Lullaby in the yellow cottonwood out front
        After the miscarriage

"It's a boy," all blood red and warm on my tummy
        One year later

A cocked black baseball cap, "Mom, where's my deodorant,"
        the teen now, asked as he rushed to the bus

At the cemetery seeking wisdom in marriage from Mom and Dad
        in the clear morning air

Dance Please

On your deathbed you wished life could have been more spontaneous. Dad always wanted routine, beds made, dishes done, Walter Cronkite on the news, meat and potatoes at six. You would step away from the laundry pile and say, "Come out, come out, wherever you are." At seven o'clock every Saturday night there was Lawrence Welk's Big Band sound. You sat by Dad on the couch, anxious for that first waltz. Was it him or you or one of us who coaxed you to "Dance please?" He stood and extended his hand to you, your bodies clasped together like a pendant, your rhythmed steps began waltzing around the living room, your ballroom. You closed your eyes, your head rested in his neck, you followed his lead effortlessly. I wondered if you smelled his scent of Old Spice. Your steps mirrored each others as you flowed across the floor. Your smile never left as his arms seemed to lift you. He straightened his body to turn you with care. You knew just what to do in his arms.

Grandma's House

When I walked through the door, my Protestant grandma would ask,
"Do you know Jesus and are you saved?"

I always thought Jesus
was there at Mass in the wafer,
and beside me
in my prayers and in Mom.

The question I needed was, "Want a cookie?"
Spicey molasses, or sour cream cookies
melted like butter in my mouth.

Grandma smelled of homemade bread and cake.

I counted on her taking Grandpa's place
in the chair that held her.
I waited for her to ask, "How was high school this week, honey?"

I was lonely that year. My best friend had moved to North Dakota.
Grandma understood lonely.
She held me against her talcum-powdered neck in her soft flabby arms.

I loved quiet Friday nights spent with Grandma. There'd be popcorn popping
in the pan and the two of us talking. She didn't have a television.

I'd wake up and walk out to the kitchen where she'd be basting eggs.
Toast was her homemade bread with crabapple jelly. She offered me milk
in a jelly jar while she drank hot coffee with real cream.

Shades of Me

Born in the shade of a cottonwood, by the Missouri river, one of many kids. Parents,
grand parents and great grand parents picnicked by this same river, same shade.
Summers were sticky, the river dirty, three fans cooled a household.
Wore hand-me-downs, played baseball with brothers and went to St. Peter and Paul's.

The river wed the prairie. I crossed the prairie to go to college and became a nun,
stayed eight years,
saw the sky forever.

Left SD prairies behind for MN forests. Couldn't see the sky. Didn't like it.
Married few compliments and paid mortgage.
Listen to spouse, two adult step children and a teen.
Learning to listen to my intuition.
Delight in hugs and pee-your-pants laughter.

Taught third graders to love stories, butterfly lifecycles and multiplication.

Sew quilts, walk miles and journal often. Smell sweet basil, cloves and cornbread.
Drink too much coffee. Phone sisters and best friends less often than I'd like.
Need to be more aware of Wall Street protests and injustice.
Member of a faith community that prays, yet need to do more for the poor.

I smile when geese and long-legged egrets fly overhead
bold crocus pop up purple
a deer wears a summer coat and winter has a birthday.
I seek the shade of a cottonwood to talk with parents past.

The Christmas Box

As the snow outside would thicken on the front porch steps,
and Christmas cards were taped around each archway in the house.

Each child in the family would begin to feel a gnaw,
of anticipated wonder would the blessed box arrive in time?

Our oldest sister Inie had married and moved south.
yet somehow she remembered her own Christmas' gone past.

When our California grandma had sent presents in a box,
to the oldest five in the family and glee had traveled round and round.

So eyes of expectation peered out the front bay window,
seeking sight of the postman and the weighty box he'd bring.

The day we forgot to track the postman's prints upon the walk,
the doorbell rang, our eyebrows raised and we younger six rushed to the door.

To see a box nine times bigger than a toaster, taller than most of us,
Hugged and framed in our front door.

We six waited as Mom set down the burly box
on the dining room table and stood upon a chair.

She opened the blessed box so tall with her largest kitchen knife.
Christmas colors tumbled out, green, red, reindeers and santas,
were found on perfectly wrapped presents, ever corner taped with care.

Each of us gently fondled the boxes one by one
checking for our name, would that one be for me?

That year in particular, not once but twice we saw,
our names on presents, smiles filled the room.

She got it in the mail, two days before the holiday it arrived,
Our sweetest older sister had put Christmas in a box.

Feast of St. Nicholas, December 6, 2011

Locket

Hinged together.

Wife	Husband
Protestant	Catholic
Lover	Lover
Mother	Father
Svelte body	Big stomach
Diets with	Dieter
Too many babies	Too much working
Smoker	Smoker
Dance with me	I will

Dread

Not daily but often enough she would enter our house by the back door.
Aunt Ruth always came with Uncle Morrie, Mom's favorite brother.
Ruth was heads, Morrie was tails, of the same coin.
Aunt Ruth, like a coyote nearing a hen house, could scatter a flock with her verbiage.

"Your shirt's wrinkled, did you wear that to school? Or "I hope you saw daughter Susan in the
Capitol Journal, front page as homecoming queen." As a grown high school senior, if I saw a
black Lincoln Continental, with door handles that faced inward,
open outward, I would hide.

Her tales were always taller. Even though Mom could have boasted that her children were in
honor society or home coming royalty, her voice went silent when Aunt Ruth entered. My aunt's
stories bluejayed louder than Uncle Morrie's, though he owned his own typewriter business.

Aunt Ruth, a nurse, worked outside the home, before most women did.
My mom stayed home with her big brood, with no help from stern introverted dad.
Did that make Ruth the alpha female? I wished Mom had spoken up to her,
blown our family horn of accomplishments in Aunt Ruth's presence.

Mom, like the brave dog at the door, would greet and stall Ruth and Morrie
just long enough for us to scatter. She took the buck shots in order to see her brother. He'd call
her "Gracie," and ask "How was your day?" As I peeked around the chair I would see Mom's
smile the minute she stood beside her Morrie.

Walt and Gracie

(to the music of Thelonius Monk)

Starlight moonlight
      Hope to see a ghost tonight.

Dad, with your girl with
      the gorgeous legs

      Mom
          Your Gracie

Not enough Bennie Goodman
For you two lovers

Just the War Effort,
Night Shift at Lockheed
And babies, too soon, babies

Inie, then Norma
Sandy, Jim then Bill,
Marge, Kathy, Ralph,
Mark, Tim then Ken

Step, step, turn, glide across
      The living room with Walt
          Waltzed together

Smile and a wink, like you used to
      You two lovers

Star-spangled,
      Navy hats and nylons on the line
          Signs of a hero and a heroine

The Hall Light

All night
the bright light
led us down the hall.

Past open stairway
it banished
intruders
as we hurried
to the toilet.

Upstairs,
three rooms,
open doors,
bathed
in hall light.

Brothers at one end,
three sisters in the middle,
parents at the other.

A sister's warmth
beside me
helped
with the winter chill.

The hall light
led me
when sick,
or nightmare driven

to Mom and Dad's threshold
quick tiptoe away.
"Can I sleep with you?"
"Crawl in," Mom would say.

Tracks

Railroad tracks mark the land next to the county road like a birthmark on the arm.
Cold steel rails, parallel lines pounded by laborers with spikes rooted in wood.

I wonder where their vanishing point leads as I look down the line.
They connect us to our past, to our great grandparents, grandparents, parents.

Oak, cottonwood and birch wave to the engineer, the only traveler along the line.
These days he doesn't carry passengers, mostly lumber, oil, and scrap metal.

Red engine connected to hopper, tank and freight cars once carried my family.
Great grandparents moved a family of nine from Iowa to South Dakota.

My grandmother, just fifteen, looked out through cattle car slats with sooty face.
Her little sister wrapped arms tightly around her leg for comfort.

Nine traveled the tracks from Lawler, Iowa to Armour, South Dakota to a new farm.
Opportunity opened reservation land, cattle would be their cash crop.

Blizzards covered the rails while cattle froze that winter of 1902.
My family lost everything.

Less to pack, they again filled the cattle car, sad faces looked out.
The tracks led them, to their new home in Wagner, South Dakota.

My grandmother met a man at the depot along the railroad tracks.
Yearning, smiles, lipstick and some whiskey brought two Irish together.

The tracks led them to Morris, Minnesota, a passenger car carried two who became one.
Tracks led them back to Wagner, so a grandmother could midwife dad's birth.

Tracks carried my Dad to Yankton College where he met my mom.
Tires took them to California where their first child was born during WWII.

Tracks like varicose veins run less wanted across this country.
Their vanishing point mysterious as the saints of our family.

Ode to My Ancestral Quilt

For Mom, Aunt Inie and Ruth Bramhall

Mother's Love is your name. You were hidden in a closet until 2004 when I found you. While searching for my roots, I had traveled to visit one of your makers, my Aunt Inie. She danced with you down the hall and into the California sunshine, unfinished she unfurled you, all forty-two squares of top quilt, as proud of you as Betsy Ross of her big flag. "Your mom and I sewed this when I was ten and your mom was twelve. Our Grandma, your Great Grandma Eernisee, sat in a rocking chair and worked with us. We sewed every stitch by hand."

I can see you held by two little girls more often than their dolls. They created you with the care they'd give to doll clothes. In 1930 there was no time for something so impractical as making doll cloths. They were given a higher calling to create something that would give warmth to their family in a biting winter. You gave them joy when puzzle pieces fit together and took shape. You are ingenious! The octagon shape of one patch became the bowtie shape in another. You loved hearing little girls' glee, "Grandma look there's the bowtie!" as you laid across their laps like the family cat.

Frugal is your middle name. No fabric was purchased to make you. You came forth from the womb of family love. Worn fabric from every member held you together. Shirts from Great Grandpa Eernisee and Grandpa Gilkerson are dotted with ash burn. Great Grandma's favorite red and white checked apron is sealed with a summer jelly stain. Green checked, the favored long skirt of Grandma Gilkerson, tickled her ankles as she walked to church. In the front room the silky orange twirled Mom in her dress and bloomers those last days of the 1920's. Inie spun on the front porch in her dress of pink and gray.

Your colors blend as beautifully as nature. The dark blue and tan square add the mystery of twilight over a prairie near Armour, South Dakota. The wrinkled green in another square seems as off color as a toad in Grandma Gilkerson's garden.

You still know how to make men and women smile as your squares make patterns, the softness of your caress touches laps and warms. Your beauty is ageless as my aunt's smile. I told her I would finish you.

Eight years later you brought two middle-aged women together. We too are friends like sisters. You allowed us the joy of feeling your silky and rough, sometimes smooth texture in our fingers the fall of 2012. We sandwiched you together with batting to a vintage creamy cotton with pink floral print. We wanted to make you stronger and give you longer life. We sewed and knotted you with silk thread of blue. You reminded us to laugh and share stories as you did my aunt and my mom. Our signature is sewed in thread that outlines two nearly invisible bowties to the back of your floral cotton.

Finished you have another mission. In tears I ask you to bless the person who needs you most. Please bless them with Mother's Love like healing hands as they lay under your warmth. Bless them with memories of Mom. But more, as a good woman, give them your protection as you did two little girls.

A Memorial to Dad

"Death doesn't end a relationship,"
the nun said a year after your too-early death.

One year of numb.

My list of gones that first year
After your death:

Welcome home hugs
Your smell of Old Spice aftershave.

"How was college this week?"
"Come have breakfast
at Country Kitchen with your mom and me."

You as a Eucharistic minister
giving us communion, a small wafer of bread in our hands.
One of only a few lay people to do this,
besides the priest.

Guidance counselor at Riggs High School.
What about that child you counseled off the edge of suicide?

What about your high-school-age sons?
Who will counsel them about
Their college choices, A.C.T. scores, drinking, girls?

How does a relationship after death work?

The second year after your death
things I wished I'd said:

I'm proud of you
for earning your Master's Degree
in Guidance and Counseling.

You listened until I found words,
"I'm terrified of algebra."
"I have no date for the prom."
"What are my talents?"

You took me to Piggly Wiggly
to buy my first box of tampons.
I was embarrassed.
You paid for it like bread.

I'm learning to like September.

Why Do We Lose the Good?

Like running in the sprinkler, swimming pools,
       sherbet at the Zesto and Dad.

When did you lose Dad?

Summer was barely over and I was still a girl
       not out of college.

Does autumn scare you?

It's unannounced and arrogant like death.
It doesn't give a damn if you're not ready to let go
of monochromatic green or innocence or his wisdom.

It's all wind-tossed and driven.
Leaving dried leaves strewn on the ground like Mom,
my brothers, sisters and me.

Is there anything good about autumn?

It takes thirty four years
to stand tall and deep red and bright yellow
as a son's hair to see some good in it.

Remembering Ruth

For Ruth O. Bramhall 5/8/1940 - 1/19/2014

Pale blue February sky, dotted in cotton
The color of a newborn's flannel blanket
Like the two patchwork quilts we made my grandchildren.

We'd sit at your small kitchen table after I arrived
Ted would serve us coffee and a chocolate treat, tell a joke, then leave
You'd ask, "How are you, dear?"
Conversation came before the sewing project.

We'd talk of books you were reading,
Laugh at your librarian days, "Do you have any books on tree frogs or testosterone?"
You'd tell me, "You need to compromise in marriage."
We'd cry over my daughter's divorce.

You'd tell me, "Eat good chocolate for a treat."
You gave me a lovely Italian ceramic creamer.
You said, "I'll bring the dice game and prizes," the 100 degree 4th of July day
We all stayed inside.

You tore fabric straighter than I could cut it.
"This square of dark blue and tan adds the pizzazz the quilt needs," you said.
 Remember the fall we hand-tied the backing to my family's heirloom quilt?

Today, I heard the single note of a blue jay's call.
I looked out the window and saw her feathers of variegated blue,
As she danced in the bare branches of the neighbor's lilac bush.

Carol Mae

December 20, 1924 – February 3, 2015

Fleshy hand rests still as ice
on the sheets blanched white

"Wake up razor wit
Wake up stories of dancing to the Big Band sounds
Wake up nurse of many, anticipating needs."

"I'm glad I had my run when Benny Goodman
played his music," her words chime in my head.

Gone soda fountain drinks,
tokens for the St. Paul street car,
paper thin pork chops your butcher dad brought home
and Kate McNearny, your Irish Grandma.

Gone too, worry over your trombone-playing husband,
all your St. Kate's Nursing Class of '46.

Your legacy, four children you taught to go to Mass.
Friends, you set out coffee, creamer and apple nut muffins for.
Countless people you prayed for and now they pray you home.

The Hug

For Jill and Jenny

Jenny stands up from her bed
Now weakened by the cancer
Beside her older sister.
Though one is taller, the two see eye to eye.

Reconciliation

Long years of tension,
Jealousy,
Anger,
Rivalry

Melt into

The hug

Shorter arms envelope
Her older sister's neck
Jenny's head rests on Jill's chest
Between their tears… whispers.

"I love you."

Morning Light

For Peg and Bill

Streams across the page through crystal front window
      A shadow follows the pen strokes

Light is welcome after the dark of her closed coffin

My face brightens, toes warm
The pound weight on my heart lifts
As I sit in the favorite sage green recliner

I wonder, "Is this a classical note sent from heaven
By her newest saint?"

Retreat Prayer at Table

Today she will not serve a guest their plate
no steamy chicken with sauce, coleslaw with cranberries for color
to put in front of each guest.
She will not offer, "Bless us O Lord," or "Coffee or milk?"

She will sit with relaxed back and allow
another to brush her shoulder
put a plate full of good food
in front of her.
"How was your day?" "What do you do?" She will ask or answer.
Smiles will cross the table, bread will be passed.
Music will linger like fountain spray.
She did not plan this dinner, another did.

May the retreat words to follow
                              lift us
like the kindness across this table.

I am

I am the kid wrapped in broken branches
of our summer wigwam in Bubba's backyard.

I am the dirt floor that upholds two little girl's bare feet
whose toes touch in this nest that holds secrets.

I am the daughter of a mother with bags under her eyes
too tired to sing lullabies to her seventh child.

I am the little sister who sleeps with older sisters talking of
Bermuda shorts, smoking out the window and my brother having sex.

I am the adult changing the color of her scarves
green for compromise with her teen, red for assertion with a spouse.

I am the horsehair brush dipped in sapphire blue
painting a jay onto a branch bowed in snow.

Another Road

If I were another on the road
I would have married younger
A man my own age with ego issues.
Had more children. Did daycare in my home. Taught fewer years.
Been a righteous SD Republican. A fundamentalist Catholic.
Had a home with east-facing windows. Never written a poem.
Been no more happy than if I'd
Been a nun
Lived in a third world country.
Married older
An older man with ego issues.
Had only one child and two stepchildren.
Taught thirty years. Got a Masters degree.
Been Liberal in politics.
A lover of all faiths. A recovering Catholic.
Live in a home with east-facing windows. Writer of poetry.

Depression

The constellation around which
A family is grouped.

Blinding

For brief moments after each child's birth
Attention left

Your illness

Depression again gathered us
A once brilliant cluster

Blacked out

Ode to Pasta

For Art

I.

"What wine and pasta cannot cure
There is no cure for,"
Is the phrase
Hung prominently
Behind the *Bertizoni*
Gas range in the home
Of one well-known,
(In his family anyway,)
Italian chef.

Before the fork turns…

A mound of semolina flour
Filled the center
Of the counter.
A nest cupped out
In the middle
Held cracked eggs.
The pasta maker
Kneaded the dough,
Kneaded the dough.

Rolled the dough,
Cut the dough
Into thin strips
Draped on chairs to dry.

Then when stockpot boiled
And garlic had been cut
Into fragrant tiny pieces
And olive oil was
Poured an inch deep
In the saucepan and simmered

The blessed strips
(Descendants of Marco Polo, who brought the noodle
From China to Italy)
Filled the pot,
And cooked for four minutes (for fresh pasta)
To eleven minutes (for dry)
Until *al dente*
(with a slight nerve).

II.

After an exhausting day
Of teaching third graders,
Or demanding day of
Tests and tennis
In high school,
This family delights
When the aroma
Of pasta rises off
Bubbling stock pot,
Filling the house
With a scent
Like grandma's yeasty bread dough,

Resurrecting energies
Once flagging
With hopes of what's
To come.
Fork twirling strands
Of angel hair
Drenched
In extra virgin olive oil
And garlic (*aglio e olio,*)
Dusted with *parmeggiano.*
A sacrament
To the weary.

Now,
As the fork turns,
At a table
Set with Italian pottery
And crystal glasses filled
With Merlot or Pinot Grigio,
Smiles fill faces,
Stories begin
And fathers, mothers,
Daughters, sons
Like Kings, queens,
Princesses and princes
Dine.
"*Buon apetito!*"

I Sang Mother

for Benjiamino Maggie

Yellow, your favorite color, paints the maple in the front
the cottonwood beside it plays percussion.

Just like that fall day eight years ago
first time I sang mother.

Red bled from maple the day you left
ten weeks we bathed in your color.

We never knew if you were girl or boy
your name we knew and do still.

The wait was long for you little one
you sang hope to a couple persistant.

Winter white the canvas color of your brother
will never change my love of yellow.

Quickly By

The window open to the dark morning air.
A pattering of lightweight rain on hardened ground
like light feet on the kitchen floor.

Your child days, your giggles and your gains
your fear of bugs, your bad dream pains,
patter quickly by.

I remember the summer of your firsts.
First words, then tottered steps,
first trike, first time your ball on bat met.

Now a two-wheeler is parked in our garage
and another woman bids you "Welcome,"
as you hear the bell and walk through the door, son.

tuck in time

for Alessandro

The little boy asked his Mom
"Who will tuck me in?"

She replied, "Mama."
He turned to brush teeth with a grin.

They lay together
his torn green blankie,
the patchwork quilt she'd made him,
tucked to their chins.

She asked, "Anything you want to tell God?"
"I didn't keep a promise
to play with a friend."

They sent it up in a fingertip bubble
for God to lessen the six-year-old's trouble.

The mother stroked his soft hair
and laid there
a few minutes more.

In the quiet
he felt her kiss
brush his cheek.

"Night, night,
I love you."
She shut the door.

My Red Cap

It's like a friend I've found

At day's end it's still with me

As I roll on the ground.

Some days its full of leaves and hay

Cuz outside we go,

I stick it deep inside my sleeve

It keeps me warm you know.

I put it on when we leave for school

Now that I am three years old.

I can put it on by myself

Especially when it's cold.

Imprints

Little foot, Big foot

Imprints on a frosted snow

Small now, too soon grown.

Our Anchor
For Mrs. Fisher

Tug-of-War
Fisher VS. Springer
May 29, 2007

Rain and excitement build!

Mrs. Fisher, our anchor
Behind us
Hannah, Allison, with her,
At the back

Alessandro, Khalid and Jordan
Up front
Facing
Mrs. Springer's class

Heavy, rough, thick rope between them.

McCarthy blows the whistle!

U h h h h h

All arms p u l l i n g

Her Capri pants s t r e t c h i n g

She's our anchor

For our third grade class

U h h h h

Rope taught as our muscles
P u l l i n g,   P u l l i n g

Across the line

We Won!
Thanks to you!

The Warrior

For Alessandro, age 11

S w i s h,   w a c k,

    S w i s h,   w a c k

The stick he wields as tall as he

        His ready sword

Cuts off

    The white puffed heads
    of the

D a n   d e   l i   o   ns

Surrounding him on all sides

        Of the backyard

The Warrior

S w i s h,   w a c k,

    S w i s h,   w a c k

Cuts down a swath of

       Ten

          Twenty

               Hundreds

Of the dreaded white w e e d s

       H u f f f f, his tired sigh

Who will win?

Weeds or Warrior?

My money's on

    The Warrior

Magical

The smallest tree tips left
At the end of the line
Of six pines in his backyard.
The now young man, when four,
Called it the "Alessandro tree."

Mama and son would sit beside this tree
Within the Hundred Acre Woods,
Where every tree had a name,
"Daddy tree," "Mama tree," "Laura tree," "Luke tree,"
"Grandma Gretchen tree."

The two would sit on powdered snow
In quiet conversation
With their wooded friends.

Eleven years have past now,
The young man states to his mom,
"Let's get outdoor lights
And light up the backyard tree!"

Braving below-zero temperatures,
With ladder and lights in arms,
They trudge across snow
Towards the shortest tree.

His frozen fingers untangle lights.
She holds the tripod ladder.
Agility moves up the steps,
Strings of lights across his shoulders.
Stretching he catches lights to branches,
Steps back down and together,
They move the ladder round and round
The branches of the eight-foot tree.

She turns to him, "You do the honors."
He plugs the thick orange cord into the back porch socket.
Into pitch dark night leaps light
Purples, yellows, greens, reds.
He raises up his gloved hand
And gives his mom a high five
And then, a hug.

September

My young boy is becoming a young man.
As he opens high school doors
he walks away from us a bit more.

He still hugs us at the backdoor before leaving for the bus.
When the garage door is up, he waves goodbye and doesn't look back.
He asks before leaving, "Do I look dorky?" when he spots a new pimple.
After homework he builds a Lego starship or rides his bike to a friend's.

Still next year he'll drive a car and take a girlfriend to the movies.
Help me note his broader shoulders, and trust change.

Bless You

God.

For forsythia's yellow grin
no longer afraid to smile

For shy green nail polish
on pubescent tree fingers

For magnolia's blush

The return of wood duck's helmet
penciled brown

And a teen's first date
with a tennis racket

Acknowledgements

I am grateful for my women's writing circle, Jill, Jacqueline and Ruth. Their encouragement pushed me to keep writing and pursue further studies at Hamline University in St. Paul, Minnesota. My Hamline instructors and poets themselves, Margot Galt and Deborah Keenan, gave me needed direction and support. After retiring from teaching, it was my poet/teachers at the Loft Literary Center, in Minneapolis, especially Thomas Smith, who kept me on the writing path.

Finally, I want to express my deeply felt thanks to my spouse Art, who was the catalyst, encouraging me to put my poems into this book. Also, to my writing coach and fellow poet, Victor Klimoski, who helped me discover two words I had never known, "My book."

Made in the USA
San Bernardino, CA
05 April 2015